SLATTERN

Kate Clanchy was born in Glasgow in 1965 and educated in Edinburgh and Oxford. She won an Eric Gregory Award in 1994. She lives in the East End of London, and works as a schoolteacher.

SLATTERN

Kate Clanchy

Chatto & Windus
LONDON

First published in 1995

5 7 9 10 8 6

First published in Great Britain in 1995 by
Chatto & Windus Limited
Random House, 20 Vauxhall Bridge Road
London SW1V 2SA

Random House Australia (Pty) Limited
20 Alfred Street, Milsons Point, Sydney
New South Wales 2061, Australia

Random House New Zealand Limited
18 Poland Road, Glenfield
Auckland 10, New Zealand

Random House South Africa (Pty) Limited
PO Box 337, Bergvlei, South Africa

Random House UK Limited Reg. No. 954009

Papers used by Random House UK Limited are
natural, recyclable products made from wood grown in
sustainable forests. The manufacturing processes
conform to the environmental regulations of the
country of origin

A CIP catalogue record for this book is available from
the British Library

ISBN 0 7011 6332 1

Typeset by SX Composing Ltd, Rayleigh, Essex
Printed in Great Britain by
Mackays of Chatham, PLC, Chatham, Kent

for Joan and Michael Clanchy,
their lodgers, and assorted wildlife

ACKNOWLEDGMENTS

I am grateful to the magazines and newspapers in which the following poems first appeared: *Ambit* for 'Trying on Clothes' and 'Designs', *The Independent* and *The Observer/ Arvon Anthology* 1993 for 'Men', *The Scotsman* for 'The Aerialist', *The Sunday Times* for 'Slattern,' *The Times Educational Supplement* for 'The Pair of Them', 'Timetable', and 'I Can't Argue With It', *Poetry Review* for 'For Absent People' and 'Mitigation', *The Rialto* for 'Pathetic Fallacy', 'Overnight', and 'Double Take', and *Writing Women* for 'Secret' and 'Men from the Boys'. Several of these poems appear in *Anvil New Poets 2*, edited by Carol Ann Duffy (Anvil Press 1995).

I would like to acknowledge the impetus to write given me by the playwright Stephen Clark, the inspiration and invaluable encouragement of Carol Ann Duffy, who caused me to continue, and the moral and practical support of my colleagues at Havering Sixth Form College. I am grateful to the Society of Authors for my Eric Gregory Award. This text has benefited greatly from the critical eye and immaculate ear of Colette Bryce, and the nips and tucks of my splendid editor, Simon Armitage.

Contents

MEN

I like the simple sort, the soft white-collared ones
smelling of wash that someone else has done,
of apples, hard new wood. I like the thin-skinned,
outdoor, crinkled kind, the athletes, big-limbed,
who stoop to hear, the moneyed men, the unironic
leisured sort who balk at jokes and have to blink,
the men with houses, kids in cars, who own
the earth and love it, know themselves at home
here, and so don't know they're born, or why
born is hard, but snatch life smack from the sky,
a cricket ball caught clean that fills the hand.

I put them all at sea. They peer at my dark land
as if through sun on dazzling waves, and laugh.

TIP

Get a hat, a homburg, keep
it on in bars, tipped
so just your profile shows.

Imply a smile, one-sided. Perhaps
a scar to hold it.
Seek out the half light, stand

oblique, a silhouette. Smoke
a blue edged trail
in icy air, by a lamppost, let

your few sharp words intensify
to clouds. Be lean.
Be leaning on the bar I plan

to enter. Irony's the ice I keep
my dreams in. Drop
some in your whisky. Hold it there.

DESIGNS

Since the tragic death of your young wife
in that sudden conflagration of bush grass
on the curve of the coast road, since I attended
the closed-coffin funeral in my netted hat,
sent the tender, blotted letter you smoothed
with your square fingers to better feel
its understanding, since our holiday in Scotland
where you learned to love again, I have
applied myself to the plan of our dream house.

Our lounge, wide as the deck of a ship, runs
the length of the sea-view terrace, done out
in terracotta with a border of Greek keys.
The chairs are laid-back, Lloyd Wright, accessories –
largely chrome. Outside, at present, are ponds
and prairie grass. I am calling to ask your opinion
on the position of the porch swing, and if
that grass with its grand sweep of dry clean blades
could, in some small way, distress you.

THE WEDDING GUEST'S STORY

Shortly after ditching me, a matter of weeks,
in point of fact, she bought a remarkable
backless dress and got hitched to an ex-army chap
who climbs up rocks on Sundays: not the sort,

that chap, if I might explain, to stop for stragglers
or to soak up sun. He'd strike for the top
in skin tight kit, lycra shorts and pick, straining
straps around the crotch. In spite of which,

I took the half-meant invite straight, sat tight
throughout, let that dress flash a foot of flesh
to the hushed cathedral, and in my mind
I slowly climbed the low, secret steps of her spine,

swung for a while on my rope in the tuck
of her waist, scrambled sweating, swearing,
over the slopes of her shoulder blades,
to slump on the summit, weak, sobbing with loss.

A MARRIED MAN

The married man dreamt last night
of a house that someone'd left him:
the sort of house you have in dreams,

a thousand rooms, one corridor. He wandered
round alone, he told me, smiled
his quiet, inward smile. *And found*

*the secret garden, high walled, locked, odd
velvet green. There, a window looked
towards the ocean.* He flexed pale hands,

I had, he said, *the key.* His wife touched
their girl asleep, a lush and heavy animal,
and watched him, knowing, satisfied.

GULL

This is how a man looks
who's lost his wife to someone else,
learned the kids were never his,
and, still, forgives:

a gull so soaked with oil
it thinks that gulls are born like this.
A huddled shape with eyes
like cysts, too dulled to tug

at matted frets of feathers, rigid tail,
that shrugs its clotted wings
at flight, or hunches them,
high-collared, shifts its narrow skull

to eye you sidelong, opens up
its sticky bill as if to let you know
that ships come often
with such cargoes, and by day.

THIS TIME

Robert will winter in Acapulco, jump
on the goods train that rattles his heart.

He's stayed too long in his steep city,
seen May sour to June dank as winter,

spent a night too many out with the lost boys
downing old aches halved with whisky. So,

Rob's off, come that last grand, to where a man
can live out a year on one good dollar alone.

Drink to him now, slumped by a cactus,
lifting his glass to the girls in Mexico.

THE FLAUTIST

Lord, let the flautist get to Ireland
with faith, combed quiff, cheap flute intact.
Let Ireland stretch wooded arms

to greet him, fold him close in a pub
where men hunch in dark coats. Let their feet
start to twitch to the beat of his boot

on the greased wood boards, let them turn
from their beer to hear a tune (learnt
in the interim from a driver or a hermit) form

from the dance of his black-rimmed nails,
whistle from the gaps in his milk-toothed grin.
Lord, let everyone sing. And later,

flushed, with a fold of fivers in his pocket,
send him down to the sea with a barmaid;
let him taste the salt and the roaring silence.

I met him in the city where he squatted
and busked for the price of a passage to Larne.
He said he was nineteen, Lord, was clearly lying.

THE AERIALIST

Having finally dined with the aerialist,
I found him just a college gymnast,
fresh pressed East Coast boy dismissed
from frosty Dartmouth February last,

distinguished just by his wish to kiss
the topmost stripe of the circus tent, sniff
sugar mixed with sawdust, trodden grass, and seek
the chalky hand of the Only Candelabra Girl.

Let me lift my glass and drink to the quirk
that lets him fly, slick in tights and lycra,
nightly through the Gods. I shall crick my neck
to see him spin his new wife high above me,

her roped mouth, her spotlit nose, and
candles in her fingers, candles in her toes.

MEN FROM THE BOYS

Imagine this man as a lonely boy:
at the biscuit-smelling, sour milk stage,
shirt misbuttoned, strangled tie,
pockets stocked with fists and secrets.

The inky boy in the front row desk,
who writes his name, address, adds
England, Earth, the Universe, concocts
a six month scheme for their general good;

gets dressed in robes to bury voles,
makes the cat a home that goes unused
or tries to help the birds with nests;
gives over spring to crushing flies

to keep a fledgling half alive; and spends
dank winter afternoons spinning
treacle over spoons or making tapes
of private jokes with laughter

added later. This boy writes runes
in milk on library books, and *Out,*
Forbidden on his door. You know
that if you grab him now

you'll hold a bag of kicking bones.
He wants no comfort, mother, home.
He'll work the whole thing out alone.

TIMETABLE

We all remember school, of course:
the lino warming, shoe bag smell, expanse
of polished floor. It's where we learned
to wait: hot cheeked in class, dreaming,
bored, for cheesy milk, for noisy now.
We learned to count, to rule off days,
and pattern time in coloured squares:
purple English, dark green Maths.

We hear the bells, sometimes,
for years, the squeal and crack
of chalk on black. We walk, don't run,
in awkward pairs, hoping for the open door,
a foreign teacher, fire drill. And love
is long aertex summers, tennis sweat,
and somewhere, someone singing flat.
The art room, empty, full of light.

TEAMS

I would have skipped the stupid games,
long afternoons spent chilled in goal,
or sleepy, scratching, in deep field,
leapt the sagging fence
and learnt, as others do, apparently,
from dying mice, cow parsley,

if it weren't for this persistent sense
of something – like the words to songs,
sung out on the bus
to matches, like my name on lists
on notice boards, shortened
called across the pitch,

trusted by the ones who knew,
the ones with casual shoulders, cool –
that thing, I mean, that knack, that ease,
still sailing, like those hockey balls,
like sodden summer tennis balls,
right past me.

RAIN, BOOK, CLASSROOM

A storm shades the page
like a stage light, dimmed,
rain hammers hard on roof-felted tin

and the children's cheeks
are bright as Christmas.
Down the soot-soft tunnels
of their fixed dark eyes,

down tracks as fine
as printed lines, black
on the blank winter fields
of the page, steam trains

to where we've never been:
a frontier town with one saloon,
a clapboard school
with stove smoke rising,

where a storm shades the page
like a stage light, dimmed, where
rain hammers hard on roof-felted tin.

THE PAIR OF THEM

First day back,
and they wait to tell me
of their long boy's summer: how they clocked
three thousand miles in their new old car,
spent Saturdays schlepping round
kitsch Southend, drove

uninsured and smiling
to the beach at Le Touquet. By August,
their parents were Post-It notes on a trembling fridge
at noon, and the bed, unmade since June,
lay rucked in candlewick,
sunlit dunes.

And then, these boots.
These high-sided butch-toed things,
with untied thongs and lolling tongues: two pairs,
the spit, but bought, they tell me, separately.
There's nothing going on here,
just telepathy.

LONG BOOTS,

with hooks,
are in this year.
Some look to take an hour
or more to criss cross precisely
from the foot, to loop,
tighten, tug the yard
of hard-gripped
cord. And

to untie,
peel slowly from
each thigh, each calf,
wrench off leather where it grips
tighter round the heel, the instep, over
the twitching nose of toes,
takes, I'd say, a mirror,
certain music,
days.

I like
their icy, skateboot
strangeness. That girl
for instance – watch her inch
to the edge of her perch, unconscious,
lost, to herself, to us,
in her marvellous
alien
legs.

ADOLESCENTS

We bother them: we're here, and scarred, alive.
We didn't exit as we should have
on our first lost love, leave
a young head lolling in long-stemmed roses,
or five wet streaks on a hotel wall.

We get to them: we keep on breathing,
raise our battered heads to the tat
of another autumn morning.
Can walk, do, and cloud and cloud
their crisp new air with our cow-like sighing.

CAN'T ARGUE WITH IT

These boys I teach wear gold like armour.
They hold up hardened hands of rings to flick
the shivering light like knives as they sit and rock

and kick. They wear their names, short cold sounds,
on gold chains at their straining necks; cross, lock
bare arms on thin young chests and rock and kick,

and draw thin breaths through narrow mouths.
I watch their feet, as they rock and kick, and hear
them breathe and ask them why, and what, and why.

MITIGATION

We think you know the secret places,
the ones you called, perhaps, *Big Sands*,
The Den, or *Grassy Hill*. They loom up large
behind your eyes. Those hands that stroke
your signet ring, were once, like ours, blunt-
fingered, small, and clutched at grass or clenched
a stone and loved the tender, ticking throat

of panicked bird or retching child.
You watched the films, played Dracula.
That doll was yours whose head came off.
You stored her up behind the fort, the patch
of dirt around her mouth. There's something
buried in the park, a shallow grave, a rotting
thrush. You know the place. And know

the swooping railway tracks and why
we stole a child, like sweeties, from the shops.
You twitch and feel the small wet thrill.
You balked, you bottled, ran, that's all.
We heard you from the Policeman's van.
We heard your hands, the short, sharp slaps
of grown-ups clamouring to get back.

WE HAVE SOME URGENT MESSAGES

Above all, in droves, they simply leave,
one dry evening, wordless, whistling.
Nightly, the radio calls them home,
known as Jeannie, last seen . . .

No answer comes. They have stepped
from the noise to the edge of their lives,
the margin where the light seeps
under the thick curved glass that holds us in.

HEROINE

She dreams of disasters, daily, at her desk:
the clean tear of an earthquake; a vast,
relieving flood; sees her profile saved
on the lifeboat, bruises rouged across her cheek;

blinks as a thousand cameras
frame her gallant, grateful wave,
feels the furry flock of microphones
feeding on her words. Or sometimes

thinks of simpler deaths: friends,
charred outlines in the fastlane,
parents, wiped in tragic fashion,
leaving her the house, the fortune;

and while she often plans the funerals
– tissued tears, the veil, the hat –
she thinks more of the phonecalls
in the bright frail aftermath, urgent voices

sorry now, saying *anything*, dying to name her need.

SOAP

Today on the box we'll watch
a baby sleep by bombs and know
she's safe: our hero's on her corner.

Here, buttered light falls always
on the garden and envy's a prop,
a bit part on the way to love
that's marked by tongueless kisses.
I love your strength she tells the man
in fancy dress. We understand.

The children play with sadness,
loss, as if with dolls; casually
swap parents. All doors lie open.
Crims are simple, dirty folk
who shoot with blanks,
and wounds are clean. They heal.

Here the dead come back
with different faces, are greeted
unsurprised. This is the place
we dream together, our fingers
on the buttons, fiddling with time;
this place where nothing hurts.

FOREIGN

Consider abroad, how closely it brushes,
stiffens your skin like the scaly paw
of a fake fur throw when you wake at four
in a cheap hotel; creeps in sly as the hand
up your thigh on the spiralling, narrowing
minaret steps, clammy and moist as the stump
of a limb that's round as a baseball bat
but soft as the skin on the pad of cats' paws.

Think of the smells, the insecticide soaked
through your rucksack, passport; the rubbery
mould on the inside of tents; the medieval streets
with their stink like a phone box; the rain
on the dust, that stench of damp dog; the rush
of iron fresh from the butcher's; the stale
of the coppery water in temples, the yellow
ringed puddles behind great beaten doors.

And noises, the multiple clicks in your mind
like a camera; the howling of prayers
tannoyed from towers; the orders,
the bargains, the beggar's *baksheesh*; flip
flop flip of doors on buses; shrieks
from quarrels you can't understand,
buzzes and flies, the sound of the crowd
rising like water left running for hours.

Above all remember how little this touches,
how by evening it's telly, just small people
miming their hunger and rage. Remember,
against the prospect of mountains, the slice
of a city glimpsed through a window,
to measure that peering in mirrors for sun tans,
those glances in darkened windows of coaches,
searching your face for the difference.

FOR ABSENT PEOPLE:
Andreas 1965–1992

We learn to live with people we have lost:
our ex-lovers, former wives, those friends
who married wrong. They send by post
the breath of distant lives, the odds and ends
of stories we once started. We do not mourn;
don't think they're gone, they live on in files
we keep to quote to new loves, sit on the lawn
in photographs with squinting, creased-up smiles.

But you went for real and we were bereft,
not just of you, but of the words, the ways
to mark your going. You had completely left.

Just this: I dreamt of heat on your last night,
woke drenched and calm and feeling light.

RECOGNITION

Either my sight is getting worse,
or everyone looks like somebody else.
A trick of the light, perhaps, or shadows

in this dark bar with its fancy candles,
but I think the girl in hippy sandals
could turn, and in a spin of bangles,

be a girl I know but somehow younger,
her before I even knew her.
Or the skinny boy in the aran jumper,

hair in the nape of his neck like a feather,
could puff out smoke, be my first lover
pulling me, laughing, into the shower:

as if no one I knew had ever got older,
haircuts, glasses, or just wandered further
than I could follow, chose to bother;

as if through sheer short-sightedness,
I could recover, rewrite losses,
sift through face on face-like faces,

make one focus, crystallise,
pull towards me, recognise,
see themselves, once more, in my blue eyes.

TRYING ON CLOTHES

This shop plays songs we sing in dreams,
sells the sounds of country, blues,
with sand-washed silks on long chrome rails;
the smoochy stuff of smoky bars,
a past we all get sick for.

Like this: a pause, big intro chords;
girls raise their heads and walk
as if enclosed in some thick shaft of sun.
Spotlit, stars with distant eyes,
they wait for their curtain.

Half-changed I stand,
like this year's ghost in 'thirties drapes,
lift up my hands to catch the notes,
see multiplied in mirrored aisles,
myself, a silent choir, swell.

CAMBRIDGE

I think it's time it withered, let us go:
the teashops, pubs, the upright girls on bikes;
the bright young men in shadowed doorways
calling clever names in code;

this softened, cheesy, gracious place
that quaintly leans to love the lounging river,
breathe its vegetable scent;
that wraps itself in tender light . . .

It's time to say enough: it's stale,
it's done to death. Let Safeways come,
McDonald's, let concrete pour,
here where the thousand bluebells lie

and dream only of bluebells, being blue.

OUTSIDE

Rats remember routes like ants.
That one you met, that grease-thighed monster,
knows the turns in your garden path,
ways through damp November earth,
has mapped in his mind the knots, the ladder
of your elaborate trellised creeper, noted
holds in the pockmarked brick and will return,
by claw on claw, to crouch and watch,
mimic, mock, hide in the screen of lacy steam
on the sill outside your bathroom window.

Whatsmore, next time you stretch and sigh,
reach one pink toe for the brass-look tap, spot
streaks on the glass, wire whiskers, teeth,
the red eyed stare, however much you shriek,
he'll only sleek one paw through slick
spiked fur and yawn. And even if you leap
or, rather, slip or squeak from the bath,
take a stand on your worn cork mat,
and, shaking, clap to scare him off,
the chances are that he'll clap back.

PATHETIC FALLACY

You can't get drenched, however much you wish it.
You could stand all autumn on our corner
stubborn as a lamppost, and watch drains fill
and then spill over, puddles stretch to dimpled floods,
and still not feel the rain run through you,
cooling, cleaning out. Your skin's too tight to let it.

You could wait till all your clothes had shrunk
to sodden sails and both shoes had split and curled
like flowers, your hair slicked down to water-weeds,
till your eyebrows dripped clear stalactites
to tide pools in your eyes, but your heart
would go on pumping the same muddy blood around.

For rain is not relieving, nor new either.
It's our own old wet reused, gone acid,
coming down still muttering its boring song of loss.
It pisses down, it spits, it clings like sweat gone cold,
and when its fingers mock our necks, old hurts,
like blackened rotting leaves, resurface in the drains.

ALL THIS STILL

It seems that grass still grows, leg-deep,
through cracks in concrete, iron mesh, that in June
there's hay, flaxen, dry, on waste ground
and on building sites, shaded in with withered red;

that Queen Anne's Lace still nods its heads
by breeze block walls or barbed wire fence;
that bindweed reaches twisted fists
to tiny holds on rusty tins in rubbish heaps;

and on hot days that children come as ever,
wade the grass, hear the vast and rustling hush
that sucks their shouts; and stretching up
to snatch their ball, hovering in the smoky sky,

still catch the scent of summer sweat:
wind-blown, heated, meadow-sweet.

FOR A WEDDING
(Camilla and Kieran 9/8/94)

Cousin, I think the shape of a marriage
is like the shelves my parents have carried
through Scotland to London, three houses;

is not distinguished, fine, French-polished,
but plywood and tatty, made
in the first place for children to batter,

still carrying markings in green felt tip,
but always, where there are books
and a landing, managing to fit;

that marriage has lumps like
their button-backed sofa, constantly,
shortly, about to be stuffed;

and that love grows fat
as their squinting cat, swelling
round as a loaf from her basket.

I wish you years that shape, that form,
and a pond in a Sunday, urban garden;
where you'll see your joined reflection tremble,

stand and watch the waterboatmen
skate with ease across the surface tension.

POEM FOR A MAN WITH
NO SENSE OF SMELL

This is simply to inform you:

that the thickest line in the kink of my hand
smells like the feel of an old school desk,
the deep carved names worn sleek with sweat;

that beneath the spray of my expensive scent
my armpits sound a bass note strong
as the boom of a palm on a kettle drum;

that the wet flush of my fear is sharp
as the taste of an iron pipe, midwinter,
on a child's hot tongue; and that sometimes,

in a breeze, the delicate hairs on the nape
of my neck, just where you might bend
your head, might hesitate and brush your lips,

hold a scent frail and precise as a fleet
of tiny origami ships, just setting out to sea.

OVERNIGHT

Then I heard your breathing thicken,
whisper past my ear like the first
inquisitive gust of a storm on the roof,

and saw darkness press through the curtains,
mass there like burdened clouds, and felt
your fingers open in sleep on my shoulders,

settle close as the first snow lining the ground,
and a dream flicker across your eyelids,
swift as the twitch of dry leaves in the wind,

and slowly your sleep deepened, gathered,
filled the room, calm as the great feathery flakes
that spin and land, weightless, one on the other,

and your arm loosened around me, suddenly,
as a branch will yield and shed its shelf of snow,
and your head dropped, filled the curve of my neck,

just as a drift might shift, and all night
your fingers brushed my skin, steadily changing
everything, like the levelled white we saw

in the morning, the lawn expectant as an empty page.

AFTERWARDS

I watch you, your face folded back
to its lines, arms sunk to the wrist
in the laundry basket. You reach
to stretch the sheets, snap
them to quarters, hold their cool pleats

like dancing partners; dig
fingers deep in the knicker heap,
smooth crushed cloth
to the shape of my hips, drape
them neat as the days of the week;

frown, deciphering scrawls of tights,
tug each skein free to a legible line.
My nightdress swoons in your hands,
you pin it up, an angel, ghost;
stoop for your jersey, open its arms,

pause, your eyes sorting clouds,
stand where the light shapes a nave
on the lino, half humming the trail
of a tune, stroke pearls of water
from clinging filaments of wool.

I watch, remember my body,
braille to your fingers, stroke
the wayward hairs on my arm.
Unwrapped in our dirty sheets,
I dream what has happened, over, again.

ONE NIGHT WHEN WE
PAUSED HALF-WAY

I saw you naked, gazing past me,
your face drawn tight and narrow
as if straining in harsh sun,

as if standing at some crossroads
surveying faceless fields of wheat.
One hand on the humming motor

counting the strung-out poles from home.

SEX, LIKE PLANES

Despite the taxied miles,
the turns, the circling dust
disturbed in vast propellers,
the growing drone
that whines, that aches,
the weight of metal plates,

there's this: this shift,
this point called flight.
We hang absurd in air
and see the earth is barely there –
far-off, a swatch of dark soft stuff
stuck with pins of light.

SECRET

I like to see you stoop and talk to animals,
you seem so very serious and large.
For instance, whispering greetings
past my kitten's upright whiskers:

your whole face puckering
as if she were a candle you thought
you might blow out. Or that earnest dog
you brought here once,

that wasn't yours, remember?
He tap danced on his claws
across my lino. Your look
was like applause. I like to think

you'd part that dog's thick coat
without disgust, pick and squeeze the tick,
walk on for miles across a moor,
whistling as he wove his swift path

round you like a shuttle. You'd know
scout's lore, advanced first aid,
could set a dragging, broken leg,
one handed with two sticks

and a handkerchief, or pluck
the yellow stamen of a bee's sting
from a swollen, sunburnt limb. You
could teach a flailing child to swim.

I think of you like this, knowing
animals and children, their signals
and their silences. All the secret creatures,
keeping them close to your chest.

TOWARDS THE END

A wrecked street-cat got up
and shadowed us, came home
and sat an hour on your lap
in the laundry cupboard.

You counted the lice
that massed on her shoulders,
dispassionate, calm
as a man from the census.

We made her live for a while,
had her sprayed and injected,
swaddled her stiff in a towel
as a mummy;

forced milky drugs
through her shut wax mouth.
You stroked her vellum throat
with one finger, put her shaking

and small in my arms as a bird.
She pushed out a paw
as if promising something.
We smiled when she purred.

And woke in the night
to modest hoarse snorings,
fine scratchings in corners,
her peppery smell; to an itch

on our hands that matched,
palm to palm, that reddened
and spread, opened, bled.
Ringworm, they said. Then worse,

quickly worse: a shriek like brakes
skidding, wet sick on the carpet,
queer lucid red, one bony worm
that uncoiled to a comma.

You shrugged when I screamed,
cleared it bent-shouldered,
laid her flat on the floor
as a joke-cat, steam-rollered,

but her breath kept coming,
kept lifting her skin worn loose
as a dust-rag. She was light,
she was just greasy bones in a bag.

I called to her, called *baby, love*,
reached for your hand. She made
a rusty choking sound, squeezed out
a last tiny shit like a stone, then

you turned away I think,
I know I cried.
There was not enough between us
to keep a cat alive.

DOUBLE TAKE

I imagined that you'd miss me, thought
you'd pace your hardwood floor in odd
worn socks, watch the clock sit stuck,

get late to work, type my name *caps lock*,
press and hold *shift/break*, miss buses, meals,
or sit with fork half-way, lost, for minutes,

hours, sleep badly, late, dream chases, shake,
send fingers out to pad the pillow, find
my hollow, start awake, roll over, hug a gap,

an ache, take a walk, damp dawn, of course,
wrapped in a mac with the collar up, glimpse
a slice of face, tap a stranger's back, draw a blank;

as I have. Each time, I run to press your face
to mine, mine, shining with imagined rain.

STILL

High pressure has ironed
the Atlantic, kept the same
air hanging until it thickens
to tissue paper laid
on watercolours. The oaks
are yellowed, foxed
like ancient books. Dead

leaves fill the paths
like packing. The cliff bathes
a battered foot where
a small baffled boat circles
in flat water. Berries group
to a fist on the sky, careful
as a monk's drawings.

I've been walking miles
over fields whose furrows
run to the cliff's edge,
down worn roads set
in hedgerows neat as beards.
Still, love hangs in my head,
and gathers, like a storm.

DARE

Yesterday, I breasted
the Atlantic while the day
stood by with held
breath, shivering on
the cusp of autumn.

The cliffs stretched
west as far as they dared.
I swam across the white
loosening noose of waves,
a little further.

DEADMAN'S SHOES

Last night your ghost walked in at two,
tall, calm as a father with his evening drink,
turned his back and sat to peel one sock off,
then the other. I hardly stirred, just matched
your usual sigh to my own intake of breath,
and slept on, near you, comforted;

but woke late and looked for your shoes
dropped in first position on the carpet.
The deadman's brogues we bought
that day in Brighton, inners stamped
with the outline of an instep. I wanted,
very much, to put my hands inside them.

SLATTERN

I leave myself about, slatternly,
bits of me, and times I liked:
I let them go on lying where
they fall, crumple, if they will.
I know fine how to make them walk
and breathe again. Sometimes at night,
or on the train, I dream I'm dancing,
or lying in someone's arms who says
he loves my eyes in French, and again
and again I am walking up your road,
that first time, bidden and wanted,
the blossom on the trees, light,
light and buoyant. *Pull yourself
together,* they say, quite rightly,
but she is stubborn, that girl,
that hopeful one, still walking.

PATAGONIA

I said *perhaps Patagonia*, and pictured
a peninsula, wide enough
for a couple of ladderback chairs
to wobble on at high tide. I thought

of us in breathless cold, facing
a horizon round as a coin, looped
in a cat's cradle strung by gulls
from sea to sun. I planned to wait

till the waves had bored themselves
to sleep, till the last clinging barnacles,
growing worried in the hush, had
paddled off in tiny coracles, till

those restless birds, your actor's hands,
had dropped slack into your lap,
until you'd turned, at last, to me.
When I spoke of Patagonia, I meant

skies all empty aching blue. I meant
years. I meant all of them with you.